Companion Guide

TARA McINTOSH

Fire Wife Companion Guide
Copyright © 2021 Tara McIntosh
www.firewifewise.com

All rights reserved. No part of this book may be used or reproduced by any means, graphic, electronic, or mechanical, including photocopying, recording, taping or by any information storage retrieval system without the written permission of the author except in the case of brief quotations embodied in critical articles and reviews.

Cover photo by Brayden McIntosh
Layout by Tom McIntosh

Cover design and interior formatting by Edge of Water Designs, www.edgeofwater.com

ISBN: 978-1-77374-094-2
Mountain Shadow Publishing
Port Moody, BC
Canada

WELCOME!

NOW THAT YOU'VE finished reading *Fire Wife: Standing Strong in Your Life, Your Relationship, and Your Dreams*, it's time to delve into the self-reflection process and set some goals.

I created this *Fire Wife* companion guide so that you could expand on the parts of the book that resonated with you. This companion guide is meant to help you go beyond the words on the pages of *Fire Wife*. Here, I want to help you put those words into actions that will lead to true transformation and lasting change. It's also meant to guide you toward your own inner wisdom by encouraging you to answer questions by thinking with both your head and your heart. From there, clarity will emerge. When we put our pens to paper, the answers we seek become clear.

Self-reflection is one of the most important things that we can do throughout our lives. When we self-reflect, we become enlightened.

When we don't reflect, we can't resolve. Whether that be an internal conflict or an external dilemma, self-reflection is balm for the soul. When we take the time to be with ourselves and to reflect on our lives, we get to know ourselves better through our self-awareness.

When we are self-aware, we not only make choices that are right for us, but more importantly we can realize how we affect those around us. What's more, when we make decisions that are in line with our integrity, our passions, gifts, and goals, life is more fulfilling—and so are our relationships.

This little book, my dear fire wife, is all about taking some time to think about your partnership, your life, and your dreams. You can answer some of the following questions, or all of them. There is no right or wrong way to travel through this book. You can work on it alone, and or you can create a community by inviting your fire wife sisters to join you on this journey, whatever suits you best. If you do feel like working through this booklet with others, such as by creating a book club, there are some tips for creating a warm group atmosphere at the back of this guide.

Additionally, your partner might be interested in working through some or all of these questions with you. It's a great way for the two of you to reflect together on matters that you might not consider otherwise. The core of *Fire Wife* is understanding one another. What better way to dig a little deeper into your lives than to toss out a question now and then? Or to sit down together over a drink and "interview" each other? Have some fun with it!

Whether you feel like discussing this book verbally in a group, writing your thoughts briefly in this booklet, or devoting yourself to more regular, thorough reflections (such as by using *The Fire Wife Journal*) I want you to enjoy yourself. Spend some time to contemplate the questions before you, chapter by chapter. This will encourage you to slow down and create a vision for your future. With it, you can deepen the relationship you have with your partner and, most importantly, deepen the relationship you have with yourself.

CHAPTER ONE

Understanding

"Sometimes all a person wants is an empathetic ear; all he or she needs is to talk it out. Just offering a listening ear and an understanding heart for his or her suffering, can be a big comfort."

~ Roy T. Bennett

WHEN WE UNDERSTAND what each person goes through in a fire relationship, frustration and intolerance dissipate.

But understanding one another does take a lot of two things: *time* and *effort*. Prior to understanding what my husband did for a living, I never really considered the magnitude of what his mind, body, and spirit went through. However, after taking the time to learn about and reflect on his profession, I became more considerate toward his specific needs, such as sleep and the time to physically recover after a difficult shift. I also came to deeply appreciate what he and all first responders do on a daily basis.

After reading Chapter One, how do you feel about what your partner does for a living? Are there fears? Any worries or stresses you need to address? Or are you comfortable with it?

_____

_____

_____

_____

_____

_____

_____

How well do you understand the positive and negative aspects of your partner's profession? Let's make a list to better examine the positives and negatives.

What Are the Positives	What Are the Negatives
_____	_____
_____	_____
_____	_____
_____	_____
_____	_____
_____	_____
_____	_____
_____	_____
_____	_____

Does it surprise you to know what they see and endure in a day? What do you imagine the impact on them is when their psyche piles up with one exhausting (often gruesome) call after another?

_____

_____

_____

_____

Does knowing what your firefighter experiences at work change your perception about your relationship or the challenges that come with it?

_____

_____

_____

_____

Do you and your partner talk about what their day was like?

_____

_____

How do family and friends who are not in the fire service feel about your partner's profession? Are they respectful, or the opposite?

_____

_____

If they are negative, how do you respond to their comments?

_____

_____

How does your firefighter respond?

_____

_____

If you have children, have they gone to the hall to spend some time with their parent to see what they do?

_____

_____

_____

_____

If yes, what did they say about their day and their parent's profession?

_____

_____

_____

_____

Perceptiveness and intuition are important traits in a fire wife or partner. Like two ships passing in the night, sometimes when we get too busy, we can miss signs of trouble with our firefighter and in our family. Your instincts or intuition come into play here. Intuition is our deep feeling of just "knowing" something that can't always be explained. Some people call it gut instinct, intuition, or perception. It's about tuning into a person's energy—if they are feeling up or down, conflicted or distracted. Your intuition is a valuable indicator of what you need to address in your life, both with your firefighter and with your family. If something doesn't feel right, check in with yourself and take action.

Are there times where you have not listened to your gut instinct, only to regret it later on? Provide some examples.

_____

_____

Fire Wife Companion Guide

_____

_____

When have you listened to your gut instinct about something and were glad you did?

_____

_____

_____

What check-in steps can you take, if you haven't already, to pay attention to what is going on with your firefighter and family?

_____

_____

_____

_____

Can you set aside time during the day or evening to have dinner, go for a walk, or a drive together so that you can talk about the great (or not great) things happening in their lives?

_____

If your spouse or family members are acting differently, who can you trust and touch base with in their lives to see how they are doing when they are not at home?

_____

Let's talk about your firefighter's Mind-Body-Spirit health. It has been said that your health is your wealth. Although firefighting is rewarding and fun, it is also physically demanding, mentally exhausting, and, of course, an emotionally-depleting profession. Supporting our firefighters to care for their health is pivotal, whether that is catching up on their sleep, exercising, eating properly, or giving them room to restore their mind, body, and spirit for their overall health. To keep our partnerships enjoyable, peaceful, and emotionally healthy, looking after our health as a whole is important. No one will ever regret looking after their health, but they will have regrets if they don't.

On a scale from one to ten, with one being really bad and ten being excellent, how does your firefighter seem to be fairing these days?

_____

Can you tell when your firefighter has had a particularly bad day? What are some of the signs you notice?

_____

_____

_____

In general, does your partner need some space to come down when they get home or do they like to talk about their day?

_____

_____

_____

Currently, what is your spouse's energy level and level of happiness?

_____

_____

_____

If there is stress, is there anything else going on in their life that could be adding to it?

_____

_____

_____

How do you encourage your partner to de-stress?

_____

_____

Being well-rested is a necessity, as we read in Arianna Huffington's experience. Are you getting the sleep you need? Is your partner?

_____

_____

Are there any before-bed habits that could be overstimulating you and your family, making it hard to sleep (e.g. social media, the news, coffee, alcohol)?

_____

_____

As an alternative to being overstimulated before bed, what could help you and your family relax so you can fall asleep easier? A healthy snack? Turn the TV off—maybe to turn pages instead? A warm bath? Decaf cup of tea? Aromatherapy? List your ideas here:

_____

_____

_____

_____

_____

If your firefighter catches up on sleep today, what can you two schedule for tomorrow or during the week? What are some fun and relaxing things you and your firefighter can do on one of their days off? Go see a movie? Go for lunch? Go for a walk or run? Put a note up on the refrigerator to share and keep track of ideas.

_____

_____

_____

Let's consider your firefighter's physical health. Do they go for regular checkups and tests? What supplements or regiments are needed to help balance their biochemistry?

_____

_____

_____

In addition to making catching up on sleep a priority, are there other ways the two of you can look after your physical health (e.g. exercising together, physio stretches)?

_____

_____

_____

With respect to your partner's mental and emotional health, have you noticed any warning signs recently, or do they seem to be doing well? Have the two of you ever sought counseling? Elaborate as needed:

_____

_____

_____

There are many ways that life at the hall can start to affect life at home, either positively or negatively. Sometimes it is something that can be managed or avoided, and at other times it is something that must be endured (or celebrated!). Let's identify some of these effects, as well as some coping mechanisms.

Have you and your firefighter been through any serious department dramas or politics? What was the outcome? Have you been able to move past it?

_____

_____

_____

_____

_____

Did it affect friendships in the department or morale at the fire hall?

_____

_____

_____

_____

Is there a crisis that is still plaguing you? Like my and my husband's experience with a departmental crisis, you may realize that it can be a great opportunity to refocus. We cannot control the choices or the lessons of other people. We can, however, make our own decisions to move on and better our lives. Our friend's choice changed a lot of people's lives. You have to know when it is time to move on—to send love, let go, and continue on with compassion and kindness.

_____

_____

Telephone or tell a firefighter. Who knew? But if you haven't figured it out yet, you soon will. Firefighters are a gossipy bunch. And though not all firefighters participate in spreading the good (or the bad) news, departments are certainly well-known for this firehall habit.

Were you surprised to discover that firefighters are "a gossipy bunch"? Are there some boundaries you need to set with your partner about "talk" at the hall?

_____

_____

Is gossip being addressed at your partner's firehall?

_____

What does "The standard you walk past is the standard you accept" mean to you?

_____

Firefighters can be controlling in some areas of their life, more notably when they transition from the hall, where it is neat, tidy and orderly, back to their home, where "real life" happens.

Do you find your firefighter controlling in certain areas at home? If yes, how do you deal with it?

_____

_____

_____

Sometimes a firefighter's need for control and order is linked to the unexpected events they have at work. While it may feel indulgent (or not), can you think of ways you can make their transition from hall to home less stressful for everyone, including you?

_____

The brotherhood bond can feel overwhelming and all consuming when you are new to the fire culture, because it seems as though everyone is competing for your partner's time. This close bond turns out to be a necessary one, because our firefighters' lives literally depend on being able to rely on their brothers and sisters in emergency situations.

How are you presently feeling about this "brotherhood" bond?

_____

_____

What have you found most challenging about this bond, and what do you appreciate about it?

_____

_____

_____

_____

Have you personally experienced the benefits of the brotherhood, such as help with a family project or support in an crisis?

_____

_____

_____

The "rookie" period can be a very trying time mentally, physically, and emotionally on a new recruit. However, this period of training is necessary to learn and build grit.

How did you and your firefighter get through the rookie period? Are you still going through that stage?

_____

_____

_____

_____

If so, does it make you feel better knowing that it is an essential period of their training and will improve in time? Why or why not?

_____

_____

_____

_____

_____

From their traditions and ability to have fun and cook together, what do you think families can learn from the fire family?

_____

_____

_____

_____

Is there anything else fire families do that you would like to implement into your own family?

_____

_____

_____

_____

Standing Strong Tips Chapter One:

- Determine Your Marriage Goals

- Make a Plan for Both Health & Stress

- Don't Get Furious, Get Curious:
  Ask Questions & Seek to Understand

- Implement Fire Family Traditions to Create Lasting Memories & Fun

- Use This Space to Set More Standing Strong Goals

CHAPTER TWO

Marriage and Divorce

"Forethought Spares Afterthought."
~ Amelia Barr

IT'S NO SURPRISE to those in and around fire life that this unique partnership has its challenges. However, when firefighters and their partners *know what to expect* **and** *how to deal with those challenges*, they'll not only feel better able to deal with those trials, **but** *their marriage will flourish as a result.* The irony, of course, is that for all the training firefighters do, very little, if any, hours are devoted to the stresses they and their spouses will feel once a firefighter surrenders their lives to the fire department. If there was more relationship education on the job, it might indirectly save the department a fortune when it comes to stress leave, rehab, or costly accidents.

Have you noticed a higher-than-normal separation and divorce rate in your firefighter's department?

_____

_____

_____

_____

Why do you think some fire marriages end in divorce?

_____

_____

_____

_____

Are you close to anyone in the department who is currently going through a divorce?

_____

_____

How is it affecting them?

_____

_____

_____

Can you understand how the spouse of a firefighter can feel neglected? In what way?

_____

_____

_____

_____

Do you feel your spouse's department is evolving when it comes to interpersonal relationships and mental health? Elaborate.

_____

_____

_____

_____

What has challenged you personally about being in a relationship with a firefighter?

_____

_____

_____

_____

How have you worked through or overcome some of those challenges?

_____

_____

_____

When the Daily Mail (August 2014 survey) asked 2,000 UK men and women who had gotten divorced if they'd ever regretted their decisions, a whopping 50% of those who divorced said they had regrets. Any time we're faced with life's big decisions exercising foresight, especially in matters that could later cause regret, is a good thing.

How did reflecting on the section "Divorce and a Look into Its Future" make you feel?

_____

_____

_____

_____

Do you know anyone who has gotten a divorce only to regret it down the road?

_____

_____

_____

_____

_____

Why do you think so many people believe the grass is greener on the other side of the fence when it comes to a long-term relationship?

_____

_____

_____

_____

While certainly not easy, do you think it is easier to work on your marriage than to get divorced? Why or why not?

_____

_____

_____

_____

Does your partner's fire department recognize the need for relationship training on the job?

_____

_____

How do you think relationship training on the job could help firefighter partnerships?

_____

_____

_____

_____

How do you think relationship training on the job would benefit the department overall?

_____

_____

_____

_____

Do you find the top ten truths about a fire marriage to be accurate for you? Which ones, if any, are not? Are there any truths you would like to add?

_____

_____

TARA McINTOSH

Fire Wife Companion Guide

Standing Strong Tips Chapter Two:

- Keep the Big Picture in Mind
- Celebrate Your Strengths
- You Are a Powerful Influence
- Make Your Relationship a Priority
- Make Yourself Your #1 Priority
- Use This Space to Set More Standing Strong Goals

CHAPTER THREE

Rough Water to Smooth Sailing

"The gem cannot be polished without friction, nor man perfected without trial."

~ Chinese Proverb

SPENDING YOUR LIFE with another person is truly an art form. In order for couples to thrive and have their needs met, one needs to not only fine-tune and finesse their communication and conflict resolution skills, but also make time for connection, which is the key component for a successful partnership. Each person in a relationship will have their own gifts, skills, and challenges to offer or work through. When couples commit to making improvements, they can expect to be happier, stronger, and closer as a result. With patience and practice as guiding principles, any rough waters you face together will smooth over in time.

Is it hard for either you or your partner to initiate relationship conversations?

_____

_____

_____

Do you feel you, or your partner, are more in charge of knowing the state of the relationship? Or would you say it is equal?

_____

_____

_____

What gifts or relationships skills do you bring to your relationship?

_____

_____

What gifts or relationships skills does your firefighter bring to your relationship?

_____

_____

Do you think having prior knowledge of what's in your fire relationship toolbox will prepare you to navigate your relationship back to smooth sailing? Why or why not?

_____

_____

_____

Words are very power-filled, and learning how to communicate well with your partner can help shift your relationship in the right direction. From communicating clearly and assertively to using language to encourage others, words and how we communicate them to others is a superpower in all relationships.

Of all the communication styles discussed in this chapter (assertive, passive-aggressive), which would you say you use the most?

_____

Were you brought up with a negative or encouraging and positive communication style?

_____

_____

Where do you think you need to improve in your communication style?

_____

_____

Where do you think your partner needs to improve with their communication style?

_____

_____

In the *Fire Wife* book, the language of virtues was introduced. Below is a list of virtues to enrich and empower your language: with them, you can uplift and inspire others, as well as call people back to correction and improvement. When you notice a virtue in a person, mention it. If you'd like someone to be more of something, use the power of positive reinforcement to let them know you appreciate that aspect. Using virtues on others has more impact because you are pinpointing what you see in them or what you would like to see from them. Telling someone they are considerate, empathetic, or helpful is stronger than using vague words or phrases that just say, "good job" or "you're a nice person." If you want to change lives and improve your communication style, using powerful and impactful language is the best place to begin.

The Magic Language of Virtues:

Accepting	Dignified	Honorable	Peaceful
Accountable	Diligent	Hopeful	Perceptive
Assertive	Discerning	Humble	Purposeful
Authentic	Disciplined	Idealistic	Respectful
Brave	Empathetic	Impartial	Responsible
Caring	Enthusiastic	Inspiring	Serviceable
Cheerful	Excellent	Joyful	Steady
Committed	Fair	Kind	Tactful
Compassionate	Flexible	Lawful	Thankful
Confident	Forgiving	Loving	Tolerant
Considerate	Friendly	Loyal	Trustworthy
Cooperative	Fun	Mindful	Truthful
Courageous	Generous	Moral	Understanding
Courteous	Gentle	Optimistic	Unifying
Creative	Helpful	Orderly	
Determined	Honest	Patient	

Examples that Acknowledge (to give someone, even yourself, praise or a compliment, to recognize their special inner gifts):

- You are a very *accepting* person, and I love you for that!
- I admire your *determination*. You are going places.
- Your *enthusiasm* is infectious. I love your positive energy.
- You are a very *caring* person. People are lucky to have you in their life.
- The sense of *joy* that emanates from you lifts everyone's spirit.
- I just want to *honor* you for your assertiveness. I appreciate the direct approach.

Examples that Encourage (when someone, even you, needs to be cheered on, reassured, or have their confidence boosted):

- Remember how it took a while to get your dream job, but you got it in the end? Well, you are a person who has always *persisted* and it paid off. Don't give up.
- You've always had the gift of *unifying* people in good times and bad. You really inspire and bring out the best in others.
- I don't think you realize how much your *service* to others impacts their lives for the better.
- Your *truthfulness* and tell-it-like-it-is way of communicating is very refreshing. I could certainly add more of that to my way of expressing myself.
- You've done an excellent job raising your kids. You've taught them how to be *generous* and *courteous*.

Examples that Correct (when someone, even you, needs to be reminded of a higher way of being—remember to build a positivity sandwich!)

- I've always admired your *honesty*, but at times it needs to be tempered with a bit of tact when speaking to others. You know I've always admired your candidness, and I, too, appreciate your openness at hearing me out.
- I know it's been a challenging year, but I'd appreciate you having some *flexibility* (or *patience, tolerance*) while we get through this. We've made it through other things before, we'll make it through this too.
- I know that you are a very *loyal* person, but you've been spending a lot of time with _____, and his problems. I understand you want to *help* him, but he's got to learn to help himself, too. You are a very *empathetic* person, but to stay *cheerful* you need to spend time doing things for you, as well.

Here's the real secret of getting someone to improve in a virtue: recognize a positive trait. My son, Brayden, was very shy when he was a little boy. However, he was comfortable with close family. When he was friendly with his grandmother, I mentioned his "friendliness". So, whenever we were somewhere new and he was being shy, I'd say something like, "Remember when you were friendly to Grandma? Well, you are a very friendly person. You know how to be friendly, so that's all you have to do when you meet a new person. Be your friendly self."

When you mention a positive trait to a person rather than criticizing them, even if they are just showing off that trait for a second or two, you will watch that virtue grow. Just by mentioning it, they will be driven to improve that virtue; when people hear kind and positive things said to them through acknowledgment, they will want to do it more often. The value of positive reinforcement aside, everyone wants to feel seen. Demonstrating to others that you see these traits in them will help develop compassion and confidence.

Want to see more gratitude in a person? Then when they show gratitude for even one second, tell them you love how grateful they are. Watch it grow and grow into more gratitude every time you mention it.

What virtue would you like to see more of with a person in your life?

_____

_____

_____

_____

_____

Make it your mission then to praise, not criticize them, when you catch them committing that virtue if even just for a few seconds. Remember, the secret to growing a virtue is noticing it in the moment.

To observe the progression, have some fun and keep track of the improvement by writing down the results. You can write down your experience here:

_____

_____

_____

_____

_____

_____

_____

_____

Part of being a skilled and effective communicator in any relationship is in knowing how timing can play a role in setting yourself up for a win. When you want to solve a conflict in your relationship, coming to the table with both the issue and the solution means the problem is more likely to get solved.

Is there something you need to discuss with your firefighter this week?

_____

_____

_____

How can you set up a positive environment to talk?

_____

_____

_____

How do you think taking the conflict resolution steps discussed in this chapter (pick a good time, take notes, to name a couple) will improve the tone of your conversation?

_____

Assertive communication is a life skill that could save people a lot of personal stress and misunderstandings. Assertive communication is not aggressive communication, which is a harsher way of talking at people. Assertive communication is kind, truthful, and tactful, sandwiching constructive criticism between positive statements. When you practice assertive communication, you are letting people know how you feel and where you stand with something. When you are assertive, you live more authentically because you make choices based on your values and leave more room to spend your precious time doing what you love. Assertive communication is disciplined, poised, and builds confidence.

Do you recognize the difference between assertive communication and aggressive communication?

Are you an assertive communicator? If so, provide an example.

_____

_____

_____

_____

If not, what steps can you take to become one?

_____

_____

_____

_____

How do you think becoming more assertive would improve your relationship and life overall?

_____

_____

_____

Can you think of anyone you know whose communication style you admire? What is it about them that makes them such a great communicator?

_____

_____

_____

_____

_____

_____

_____

Setting clear boundaries with others goes hand-in-hand with the practice of assertive communication. Boundaries are essential for your peace of mind and for living a life that you love. When you don't set up boundaries with others or around situations, you can feel anxious or taken advantage of because your time is never yours, and it becomes hard to relax. You have the right to set boundaries, regardless of who it offends. When you set boundaries, you can accomplish a lot more.

Can you identify where in your life there are lines being crossed?

_____

_____

_____

_____

What boundaries would you like to set?

_____

_____

_____

What declarations can you practice over and over using truth, kindness, and a positivity sandwich to describe your new boundary? Here are some declarations help to get you started:

I appreciate that……..however……

I thank you for thinking of me…..however….

This (whatever "this" might be) is not working for me, but *this* will work for me…..

I feel hurt (caught off guard, out of the loop, unprepared) when….so would appreciate it if…..

Fire Wife Companion Guide

_____

_____

_____

_____

_____

_____

_____

_____

_____

_____

_____

_____

Are there any reasonable, win-win options you can offer to the person who is crossing your boundaries? Remember my neighbor, who kept popping in to my home at very inconvenient times? What options can you come up with for your own situations?

_____

_____

_____

_____

_____

_____

_____

_____

The more you practice setting boundaries and speaking up the more confident you will begin to feel. Can you practice reading out your new declarations while looking in the mirror? The more you practice, the more you will become comfortable with these declarations.

Who do you think will not appreciate you setting boundaries and why?

Fire Wife Companion Guide

_____

_____

_____

_____

How do you think not setting boundaries with people will negatively affect your well-being and health?

_____

_____

_____

_____

Is your partner good at setting boundaries with firefighter friends?

_____

_____

_____

_____

Can you figuratively relate to my story of the Family Fence? Elaborate.

_____

_____

_____

How do you think speaking assertively and setting boundaries will change your life for the better?

_____

_____

_____

Counseling is another useful tool that can change our relationships, and our lives, for the better. Having an impartial third person to guide you and your partner through areas in your life that you cannot solve together is a proactive way of garnering new tools and skills that improve your relationship.

Have you been to a counselor before? What was your experience like?

_____

_____

_____

_____

_____

_____

Have you and your firefighter been to a counselor? Did you find it to be helpful? If yes, in what way?

_____

_____

_____

_____

Did you learn to use some new tools you found beneficial?

_____

_____

_____

_____

How do you think a good counselor should conduct themselves?

_____

_____

What do you think the goals of good counseling should be (e.g. keeping track of progress, the goal of graduation, etc.)?

_____

_____

_____

_____

Taking a trip down memory lane can shift your perspective and thoughts about your relationship today. Identifying what you love about your partner, and your differences, too, can help you to see them as a positive, rather than negative, force in your relationship.

What qualities or quirks did you love about your firefighter when you first met?

_____

_____

Fire Wife Companion Guide

_____

_____

_____

What made you decide this was the partner for you?

_____

_____

_____

What qualities do you admire in your firefighter now?

_____

_____

_____

_____

"Vive La Difference," when translated from French to English, simply means, "long live the differences!"

How does reading the section "Vive La Difference" make you feel about the differences between you and your partner?

_____

_____

_____

_____

Do you think our North American culture encourages the battle of the sexes? Why or why not?

_____

_____

_____

_____

_____

_____

Does the French philosophy of Vive La Difference resonate with you? In what way?

_____

_____

_____

_____

In referencing "Tom's Corner," are there things you do for your partner (or family) to keep the peace? Are there things they could do for you to also keep the peace?

_____

_____

_____

_____

Connection and reconnection between couples is a vital component in a healthy relationship. When we lose our connection to our partner, we can feel lost and out of sorts with them. If connection is lost, reconnecting is about finding the North Star that will lead you back to feeling good about each other again.

Now that we've talked about communication, boundaries, and identifying our unique traits, how can we use them to learn to reconnect with our partners?

Like my husband Tom and I, are there some simple connection fixes that you have been neglecting? For us it was going away just the two of us. What might it be for you?

_____

_____

_____

_____

_____

When was the last time the two of you went away together without family and friends?

_____

_____

_____

How about planning something enjoyable, just the two of you? Write down at least five things you'd like to do, just you and your spouse.

    1.

    2.

    3.

    4.

    5.

In what ways do you and your firefighter treat each other like you are on the same team? In what ways do you not?

_____

_____

_____

When push comes to shove, do you have each other's backs? If so, provide an example or two:

_____

_____

_____

If not, why do you think that is? What obstacles are standing in the way of you two having each other's backs?

_____

_____

_____

_____

Is there something you two need to talk about or let go of, such as resentment, anger, or jealousy? This will allow you to clear the air and behave like a team.

_____

_____

_____

_____

_____

_____

Do you and your partner prioritize sex together?

Are there some conversations that need to be had so you can feel more intimate?

Is there anything holding you back from feeling safe and cherished with your partner? If there is, what conversations do you feel you need to have with your significant other using the communication and conflict resolution tools discussed?

_____

_____

_____

The Golden Rule is a simple life law: treat others as you would like to be treated. Are you conscious of the Golden Rules as listed in this chapter? Do you practice them regularly?

_____

_____

_____

_____

How does it feel when someone apologizes to you? Do you forgive easily when someone holds themselves accountable?

_____

_____

_____

_____

Fire Wife Companion Guide

When you are the one in the wrong, are you good at saying sorry?

_____

_____

How do you think most relationships would be if people apologized easily when they were wrong?

_____

_____

Are you a generous person? I don't necessarily mean materialistically. Having a generous spirit lifts people up and makes them feel cared for. How do you think a spirit of generosity affects a relationship?

_____

_____

_____

_____

_____

Between one and ten, how would you rate yourself as a generous person, with one being poor and ten being very generous?

_____

_____

List five ways you can be generous this week to those you love or to those around you (compliments, acts of service, doing favors, planning something special, helping with errands, a kind gesture, etc.).

1.

2.

3.

4.

5.

With respect to "the toothpaste wars," do you find yourself sweating the small things? If so, do you find it causes you stress?

_____

_____

_____

_____

How do you think not sweating the small things would improve your relationship and the quality of your life?

_____

_____

_____

_____

Standing Strong Tips Chapter Three:

- Take a Trip Down Memory Lane

- Make a Gratitude List

- Plan a Special Date or Get-Away Just the Two of You

- Surprise Your Partner with a Treat

- Practice Assertive Communication & Setting Boundaries for Peace & Sanity

- Set Up an Inspiring Area at Home Just for You

- Use This Space to Set More Standing Strong Goals

CHAPTER FOUR

The Predictable Stages of a Fire Relationship

"Trust the wait. Embrace the uncertainty. Enjoy the beauty of becoming. When nothing is certain, anything is possible."

~ Mandy Hale

ANYONE WHO WAS in a relationship with you prior to the relationship you have with your long-term partner had it much easier! Remembering this will often put the more mundane, and even some of the more challenging, relationship issues with your partner into perspective. They say "Things don't happen to you, they happen for you." This is because life is all about learning lessons. And when these things that are happening *for* you feel difficult to bear, remember that "this too shall pass."

What "baggage" have you brought into your relationship that may not be an accurate or a truthful way to live your life?

_____

_____

_____

What did you think of my friend Joanne's advice about "holding on" in your marriage, particularly around that 7-year mark?

_____

_____

_____

_____

Were you surprised by any of the "Interesting Facts" about marriage? Was there any particular one that surprised or stood out to you the most?

_____

_____

_____

_____

Here are the predictable stages that marriages "grow" through:

- The Celebratory Stage
- The Disillusionment Stage
- The Big Choices Stage
- The Bridge Stage
- The New Skills Stage
- The Evolution Stage
- The Juicy Peach Stage

What stage or season of life are you and your firefighter currently in?

_____

_____

_____

Are there more responsibilities or in-law issues than normal? Money lacking? Are you content, settled, and happy? What lessons can you draw from this time?

_____

_____

_____

_____

_____

How can you be patient and persevere during this time? What character traits do you feel this time is preparing and strengthening your for?

_____

_____

_____

_____

_____

Fire Wife Companion Guide

Can you relate to any of the stories in this chapter from the sections "When Your Marriage Hits Bottom," "The Winter Season of a Relationship," or "When Trust is Broken"? Can you elaborate?

_____

_____

_____

_____

_____

Was there any particular stage, tools, or steps that stood out to you?

_____

_____

_____

_____

_____

What did you think of the coping mechanism: a Psychic Separation?

_____

_____

_____

_____

Do you think this coping mechanism, also known as a "marital ceasefire" would help you and your partner during tough times?

_____

_____

_____

_____

What does 'getting real' about relationships mean to you?

_____

_____

_____

Fire Wife Companion Guide

Does my moment of realization in Whistler, that there is no such thing as a perfect person or relationship, take the pressure off for you as it did for me?

_____

_____

_____

How do you feel after reading both Chris and Marie's very different marital outcomes?

_____

_____

_____

How did you feel after reading Marie's "Standing Strong" tips, particularly that you have lots to look forward to in the future?

_____

_____

_____

_____

69

What do you wished you had known before you had gotten married or otherwise committed to your relationship?

_____

_____

_____

_____

_____

_____

_____

If asked, what positive advice would you give to a person getting married?

_____

_____

_____

_____

Fire Wife Companion Guide

_____

_____

_____

_____

Standing Strong Tips Chapter Four:

- All Partnerships Go Through Predictable Stages

- Embrace Imperfection

- Pick a Comforting Mantra(s) for When the Going Gets Tough

- Honor Your Intuition and Your Heart & Soul's Instinctive Needs

- Remember that the Seeds of Flowers You Can't Yet See Under the Earth's Frozen Surface Will Bloom Again

- Use This Space to Set More Standing Strong Goals

CHAPTER FIVE

Standing In Your Shoes

"Owning our story and loving ourselves through that process is the bravest thing that we'll ever do."

~ Brene Brown

FIRST OF ALL, have you stopped to think about how remarkable you are? You play an irreplaceable role to many people in your life, and an invaluable role to the fire department. However, as the partner to a firefighter, it's easy to feel overwhelmed, out of the loop, or that your dreams have taken the slow track because your partner's profession is so consuming. However, your reality, and what you go through, needs to be acknowledged and valued.

We bring peace and balance to our lives when we keep the big picture in mind and practice the law of order. We bring further poise to our day-to-day when we honor our feelings and then find healthy ways to discharge negative ones (therapy work, writing, and talking to a trusted friend, to name a few).

Today and from here on in, I'd like you to take some time to remind yourself of your own strength and courage. Make a list of at least 10 things that you've done that make you feel good about who you are. Include accomplishments, endeavors, travels, brave acts, and personality traits. Remind yourself of the little things you accomplish in a day. We might not be able to do it all, but we need to celebrate ourselves for doing what we can. Keep in mind that 10 things is just the beginning. Carry on to 100, or more!

1.
2.
3.
4.
5.
6.
7.
8.

9.

10.

What can you share with your partner about the harder parts of being in a relationship with a firefighter so that they can understand your perspective more?

_____

_____

_____

_____

_____

What dreams do you have about your future career, calling, or life purpose?

_____

_____

_____

_____

_____

_____

What have you sacrificed or put on hold because of your firefighter's career?

_____

_____

_____

_____

How do you feel about that?

_____

_____

_____

Does hearing about my Aunt Jean's phone call make you feel any different? Are you less anxious or more anxious?

_____

Practicing the Law of Order means that we are realistic about the future and what needs to happen first, so that we don't rush through the seasons of our life to accomplish things prematurely. Let's examine this law a little more closely.

What are your true priorities now?

How would practicing the Law of Order take stress off of you? How can it help you to "go with the flow" and be present in the here and now?

_____

_____

_____

_____

_____

How would applying the Law of Order to your life be a good investment for your future?

_____

_____

_____

_____

Practicing the Law of Order takes both patience and perseverance. How would implementing both of these virtues continuously help you to keep your eye on your dreams and goals?

Where in your life do you need to lighten up? What would help you to have a lighter heart and see some things with a sense of humor?

Can you look to any mentors who have followed The Law of Order?

Why not write a special note to yourself like I did in my journal? You can put it in a journal of your own, or put it somewhere you can see. In the future, you can read this note to see how everything works out even better than you imagined, provided you honor The Law of Order.

While you may not be able to accomplish all that you want to right now, what can you do today to get you started toward the vision you have for your life?

_____

_____

_____

_____

_____

_____

What simple rituals can you get into the habit of practicing that will help you to stay in the moment? (e.g. putting your hand over your heart and closing your eyes for a minute? Sitting outside in nature and breathing in deep fresh breaths? Spritzing your face with some aromatherapy? Becoming aware of your thoughts and routinely changing them back to positivity and gratitude?) What rituals work for you?

_____

_____

Perfectionism is a problem for too many people. Besides making us feel bad, it also takes away our joy in our little accomplishments. Where in your life can you loosen the reins of control to relieve stress or feelings of being overwhelmed?

_____

_____

_____

Think of some positive mantras you can say to yourself when you begin to feel stressed. Write them down here, and make an effort to incorporate them into your daily life, especially while you are making changes.

Mantras or Quotes:

_____

_____

_____

_____

It has been said that fear is "False Evidence Appearing Real." What are some of your worries or fears in your life right now? Take some time to sit down and dissect them.

_____

_____

_____

_____

After reflecting on your worries or fears, which of these would you say are likely not real?

_____

_____

_____

_____

If some of your worries or fears are reasonable, what safeguards can you put into place to feel better about them?

_____

_____

_____

_____

How can you replace these anxious thoughts with some realistic and earthy advice from your older, wiser self?

_____

_____

_____

_____

_____

_____

_____

Do you have a pragmatic person in your life that can help you put your fears into perspective? If so, what would they say?

_____

_____

_____

_____

What proactive things can you do to put your worries and fears away?

_____

_____

_____

_____

Because of shift work, possibly caring for children, and the shared trait of independence, fire couples, like many people, can forget to spend enough quality time together or take the time to reflect on what's going on in their relationship. To stay aware of this and to stay connected, check in as a couple from time to time to make sure everyone's needs are being met.

What are the feelings you've been having about your relationship lately? Are you living separate lives? Feeling out of the loop or like a second-fiddle? Are you dealing with insecurity or jealousy?

_____

_____

_____

_____

Having read through Chapter Five, what are some positive ways that you can deal with these feelings?

_____

_____

_____

_____

If you are feeling jealous or insecure, what action steps can you take to begin feeling more confident and fulfilled?

_____

_____

Have there been times when you felt like the second-fiddle to your partner's fire siblings? How did you handle it?

Have you learned how to deal with your partner's "mood flu," or are you still practicing? Like my mantra, "this does not belong to me," what are some ways you can or already practice to detach from your partner's moodiness?

Have you experienced any recurring emotional stress as a result of your firefighter's profession? If so, what recurring thoughts come up for you?

_____

_____

_____

_____

How do you deal with these thoughts? If you haven't started the process of dealing with and healing recurring emotional stress, what do you think might work for you? What would you like to try?

_____

_____

_____

_____

Are you able to quit mourning and start living?

_____

_____

What steps can you take toward reclaiming your joy and life? Make your plan here:

Step 1:_____

_____

Step 2:_____

_____

Step 3:_____

_____

Step 4:_____

_____

Step 5:_____

_____

Step 6:_____

_____

Did you find the section on "Healthy Ways to Discharge Feelings" helpful? Have you tried taking any of these steps (Identify Your

Feelings, Get Support From a Trusted Friend, etc.) when you have an emotional issue that needs to be dealt with?

_____

_____

_____

What virtues do you feel you have developed as a result of your relationship with a firefighter?

_____

_____

_____

_____

_____

_____

_____

Have you ever thought about just how influential you are to the health of the fire department? After all, you are the one on the other front lines. Take some time to think about this and then write down your role and why you are important.

_____

_____

_____

_____

Does your firefighter's department take the time to recognize the partners on the "other front lines"?

_____

_____

If not, how would you like to see this changed? How could it be implemented?

_____

_____

_____

Can you relate to Leanne's "Standing Strong" tips?

_____

_____

Were there any of Leanne's tips that resonated with you in any particular way?

_____

_____

_____

_____

Standing Strong Tips Chapter Five:

- Your Truth Will Set You Free

- Trust in the Law of Order

- Honor Your Feelings

- You Play an Invaluable Role to Your Firefighter & the Department

- Stay on Top of Healthy Ways to Discharge Negative Feelings

- Use This Space to Set More Standing Strong Goals

CHAPTER SIX

Moving From Feeling Like A Five To A Ten

"Happiness is the best makeup to emphasize your inner beauty and outer glow."

~ Debasish Mridha

TO SUSTAIN AND enjoy a healthy, intimate relationship, it helps to be both self-aware and accountable. It's also vital that we are open to understanding another person's feelings and needs. Fortunately, and at times frustratingly, intimate relationships will highlight where we need to heal in our lives, and also where we need to grow.

While working on and growing in our relationships makes us better and happier people, the truth is the most important relationship you will ever have will be the relationship that you have with yourself. Taking the time to uncover what could be blocking you from blossoming into your full self is at the core of *"amour propre"*. You deserve to develop your full potential and to enjoy a lifetime of happiness.

How do you feel overall about yourself and how things are going in your life at this moment? Try rating it between five (average or less than average) or a ten (optimal and happy)?

_____

_____

_____

_____

In reviewing the reasons why we sometimes don't act our best, did any of them resonate with you personally?

_____

Do you regularly take the time to reflect on your life?

If you have felt like you are living well under your potential, what life trauma, event, or experience do you think could be holding you back from living the life that you deserve and from becoming your authentic self?

What would your 99-year old self say to you about living your life half-full?

_____

_____

_____

_____

What would she say about the blocks that are holding you back?

_____

_____

_____

Knowing that you deserve to live a joyful, peaceful, and successful life, what steps can you take to launch your comeback?

Step 1: _____

_____

Step 2: _____

_____

Fire Wife Companion Guide

Step 3:_____

_____

Step 4:_____

_____

Step 5:_____

_____

Step 6:_____

_____

On the road to authenticity, we all have to figure out what is blocking us from blossoming into our full selves. For some, it may be a lack of confidence or negative thinking; for others, it might be old, unfounded beliefs, people pleasing, or abuse of any kind.

After taking some time to reflect on this, what do you think that might be for you?

_____

_____

_____

If finding out what has been blocking you is hard to figure out, do you think seeking counseling might help?

Where in your life do you feel that you are growing into more of or retreating into less of yourself? How about with other people, your job, your health, or your self-esteem? Take some time to consider this.

Where in your life have you been "playing small" so that you do not offend others?

_____

_____

_____

_____

You cannot give away to others what you do not have inside. What parts of yourself do you think need to be healed so that you can become your authentic self and heal your relationship?

_____

_____

_____

_____

It's time to brush the slate clean and begin a new chapter. What are some of the things you would like to brush away?

_____

_____

What would you like to see written in your new chapter?

_____

_____

_____

_____

_____

After reading through the section on "Assembling Your Team," what team members would you like to bring together to support you in feeling good again?

_____

_____

_____

_____

_____

Have you had any "team" recommendations through friends?

_____

_____

_____

_____

Are there any well-respected book authors or an online community you think could really benefit you? Make a list.

_____

_____

_____

_____

Do you currently make fitness a part of your life?

_____

_____

_____

If not, what can you do to get started on something you know you will enjoy?

_____

_____

_____

_____

Have you ever been tested by your doctor to see what vitamins you might be lacking in your body? This is particularly useful if you have been feeling tired and fatigued. Understanding what your body needs will improve your overall sense of well-being.

_____

_____

When you take care of your spirit, everything else in life just seems to fall into place. What activities do you enjoy that honor this very important part of who you are?

_____

_____

_____

Where in your life do you have confidence issues?

_____

_____

While making significant transformations to improve your life, do you think the "Five-Point Plan" will be useful to you? Is there anything that you would add to it to remind yourself to be both kind and patient with yourself while you make these changes?

_____

_____

_____

_____

One way to contribute to feelings of well-being and increase your energy is to stimulate your hormones and follow the DOSE of love diet. DOSE stands for: Dopamine, Oxytocin, Serotonin, and Endorphins. When any of these hormones are stimulated, you feel fantastic! Making use of these hormones will improve your confidence levels and make you feel better. Before you write out your DOSE of Love Plan (which is below), here is a quick recap of just a couple of ways you can stimulate each hormone:

Dopamine: Is activated when you check something off your check-list or accomplish something, like a goal.

Oxytocin: This bonding hormone is activated when you are with your loved ones, have a great conversation, or receive affection.

Serotonin: We can activate this hormone by counting our blessings, having a warm bath, or eating a nice plate of pasta.

Endorphins: Exercise, a good laugh, or good sex will increase your endorphins by giving you a "runner's high."

Add ideas for your DOSE plan here:

Ways to increase your dopamine:

_____

_____

Ways to increase your oxytocin:

_____

_____

Ways to increase your serotonin:

_____

_____

Fire Wife Companion Guide

Ways to increase your endorphins:

_____

_____

Self-reflection to see where we might not be contributing positively to our partnership is a must. If we don't self-reflect, we can't take accountability for our behavior, and thus our situation can't change and we can't grow. Self-reflection does not take away from your inner beauty, strength of character, or your goodness as a person. Self-reflection only adds to it.

At the beginning of the chapter, we read a conversation between a young fire wife and her fire wife grandmother. How did you feel after reading the conversation between these two? What did you observe?

_____

_____

Knowing the grandmother's response came from a deep place of love, how do you think the granddaughter responded to her?

_____

_____

_____

105

Do you have people in your inner circle who can be honest with you and who have your best interests at heart? Who are they?

_____

_____

How do you respond to them when they are honest with you?

_____

_____

How do you handle honest feedback from others after you have confided in them?

_____

_____

What parts of yourself do you think your relationship can heal?

_____

_____

Are you blaming your spouse for something that only you have control over? If so, what is it?

_____

Writing out a timeline of your past accomplishments and successes can help you appreciate what you have experienced and overcome.

Using the area below, devote a good amount of time to think about and write out your timeline. Feel free to add as many years and decades to your timeline as you wish, including your accomplishments, successes, and challenging times. Take a look to see when things were going really well for you and when things weren't.

_____

_____

Using the questions from the book, write out your answers below or go into more detail in a journal.

When did you observe times of happiness? Try to identify what it was during those times that made you feel so good.

_____

_____

_____

_____

What events changed you, for better or for worse?

_____

_____

_____

_____

When did an event or situation change your life's trajectory? How did you deal with that event?

Fire Wife Companion Guide

_____

_____

_____

_____

_____

Who are the kind, candid, truth-tellers in your life?

_____

_____

_____

_____

Do you have any negative situations or people that are currently affecting you?

_____

_____

_____

Can you link your success or failure to being around any of these people?

_____

_____

_____

_____

Has there been a turning point when you knew things had to change? Have you taken any steps toward making these changes?

_____

_____

_____

_____

If you took steps to change, how did it make you feel?

_____

_____

_____

Where are you now on this timeline?

_____

_____

Would going over this timeline with a good friend or family member give you further clarity or support?

_____

_____

We are often very focused on how we treat others, but frequently neglect ourselves. Treating yourself like your own best friend can change your life, and always for the better.

What does self-respect mean to you?

_____

_____

Where are some areas in your life you need to set some boundaries (and with whom)?

_____

_____

Where in your life have you had too high a tolerance for inappropriate behaviors?

What would it look like to be loyal to yourself?

Is there any pruning you need to do? Habits, job, relationships, lifestyles, and personality traits that aren't serving you and thus holding you back from a better life?

Are there any current relationships that you need to examine that are disrespectful toward you? What changes do you need to make to protect your self-esteem?

_____

_____

_____

What values are important to you in personal relationships?

_____

_____

_____

_____

Is there anyone you need to have an honest conversation with about your relationship?

_____

_____

_____

Are there some relationships where you need to consider moving on from or go "low contact?"

_____

_____

What does "we are all equal, but we are not all beneficial to each other's growth" mean to you?

_____

_____

_____

_____

While it can be difficult to let go of someone who is holding you back, you can take some time to review "My List" for guidance and support in helping you to make these life-changing decisions. Instead of pouring out our energies into toxic or unreliable relationships, we should focus on positive relationships that are purposeful and help us to grow.

Do you know anyone who has the "It Factor?"

_____

_____

_____

_____

What qualities make a person have the "It Factor" to you?

_____

_____

How did it make you feel after reading about the women on the beach of Croatia?

_____

_____

_____

Make a list of five women you admire and why you admire them. Think of what virtues they have that you admire and how they make you and other people feel.

1) _____

Virtues:_____

2) _____

Virtues:_____

3) _____

Virtues:_____

4) _____

Virtues:_____

5) _____

Virtues:_____

In going through the list of virtues in the book, what virtues do you feel that you are strongest in?

_____

_____

_____

_____

_____

What virtues would you like to practice and grow in?

_____

_____

_____

How can you throw yourself into practicing these virtues so that you grow stronger in them?

_____

_____

_____

In addition to making a list of women who are strong in virtues I admire, I also made a list in the section "Tips to Discover Inner Beauty" of traits or virtues that I think are stand-out qualities in a person: authenticity, positivity, gratitude, courtesy, and benevolence.

What did you think of the section Tips to Discover Inner Beauty?

_____

_____

When going through the list of the above "stand-out qualities", what choices can you begin to make that will honor your authenticity?

_____

_____

_____

What can you put into practice daily to enhance your feelings of positivity, particularly toward yourself?

_____

_____

_____

Practicing gratitude gives us an overall sense of well-being. How does it make you feel when you are thankful? How do you think it affects others when you practice gratitude?

_____

_____

_____

How does practicing courtesy make you feel? How does a culture of courtesy affect those around us? How do you think being known as a courteous person adds to a person's reputation?

_____

_____

_____

_____

Benevolent behavior can increase warmth between people, even strangers. How do you see benevolence influencing the atmosphere around you? How can you change someone's day for the better by giving them a reprieve and some understanding?

_____

_____

_____

_____

Standing Strong Tips Chapter Six:

- Self-Reflect to be Self-Aware

- Make *Amour-Propre* a Daily Habit

- Give Yourself a D.O.S.E. of Love to Feel Optimal

- Honor Your Experience

- Prune to Bloom

- When We Heal Ourselves, We Heal Our Relationships

- Use This Space to Set More Standing Strong Goals

CHAPTER SEVEN

Looking After Your Home

"Please take responsibility for the energy you bring into this space."

~ Dr. Jill Bolte Taylor

On a scale from 1-10, one being poor and ten being excellent, how would you describe the energy in your home? Why?

_____

_____

_____

_____

What was your firefighter's home life like growing up?

_____

_____

_____

What was your home life like growing up?

_____

_____

_____

_____

Have your different experiences caused any clashes or division? How so?

_____

_____

_____

_____

What does your ideal home life look like to you?

_____

_____

_____

_____

What does your firefighter's ideal home life look like?

_____

_____

_____

In combining the best of your inherited values, tone of your home, and traditions, what does an ideal home life look like for you and your partner?

_____

_____

_____

_____

What are some things you could do to enhance the good vibes and energy in your home (clean, de-clutter, flowers, music, positive words)?

_____

_____

_____

_____

Creating traditions with family and friends is what good memories are all about. Traditions are something we all look forward to; they connect and bond people together.

What are some of the traditions you have with family and friends that you love?

_____

_____

_____

_____

What are some of the influences from other people's homes, your childhood, and cultures that you love? Would you like to implement any of these into your own traditions?

_____

_____

_____

_____

Are there any ancestral traditions you'd like to continue in your family?

_____

_____

_____

What are some traditions you enjoy with your fire family?

_____

_____

We know that clutter often makes us feel disorderly and stressed. Sometimes we could all benefit from taking a page from the firefighter's organization manual.

Is your firefighter an organized person?

_____

_____

Are you an organized person?

_____

_____

How do you feel when your surroundings are orderly and organized?

_____

_____

_____

Where in your home would de-cluttering make you feel better?

_____

_____

It's easy to feel overwhelmed when you look at having to organize your house as a whole. Do you find it easier to only focus on one thing at a time?

_____

_____

Have you chosen a cupboard, closet or room you'd like to get started on? If so, where would you like to begin?

_____

_____

What is your vision for this area? How will it make you feel once it is completed?

_____

_____

_____

TARA McINTOSH

Look through your home to determine what you find either beautiful or useful. Now decide what you would like to do with what you no longer need. Donate? Garage Sale? Flea Market? Pass it on to family or friends? Have nothing in your house that you do not know to be useful or believe to be beautiful. Let's get started on your lists.

Beautiful	Useful	Let Go Of
_____	_____	_____
_____	_____	_____
_____	_____	_____
_____	_____	_____
_____	_____	_____
_____	_____	_____
_____	_____	_____
_____	_____	_____
_____	_____	_____
_____	_____	_____

Can you set some dates to have things repaired, given away, or revitalized?

_____

_____

_____

_____

Do you have a hard time saying no to things? Are you already feeling stretched? Time to de-clutter your calendar! Too many burdens on your time can leave you feeling drained and unproductive.

Make a list of things that you absolutely have to do (e.g. take the kids to soccer, go to a dentist appointment, etc.)

_____

_____

_____

_____

Now make a list of extra-curricular activities that you dread. Can you get out of any of them to free up your life and feel less stressed? If you can't now, can you make a commitment to yourself to no longer accept "obli-vites"?

_____

_____

_____

_____

Time to make a list of your top five values and what is important to you. This list will help you to focus your time and energy on things that matter to you. This way when you say "yes" to something, it falls in line with your values.

1) _____

2) _____

3) _____

4) _____

5) _____

One way to combat stress in your fire home is with a plan to start the day off right. Whether that is getting up early to exercise or have quiet time to yourself, how does starting the day right look to you?

Fire Wife Companion Guide

_____

_____

_____

What plans and preparations can you make in advance to get your day started off right (e.g. getting the coffee pot ready the night before, pack your lunch, get clothes organized)?

_____

_____

_____

What special preparations can you make in advance for when unexpected events interrupt the flow of your day (longer than normal wait in the doctor's office, traffic)? This can be something as simple as keeping your purse stocked with a snack, water, pen, and paper when you have a delay in your day.

_____

_____

_____

After a weekend, I like to take it easier on a Monday and don't put much on my schedule. Consider what each day of the week is like for you, and organize your week in accordance to your natural rhythms. For example: On Monday I like to relax with the family, Tuesday grocery shop, Wednesday appointments…

_____

_____

_____

_____

_____

_____

_____

Getting your kids to help out around the house when they are young is a good habit to get into. When our kids help out around the house, it leaves us more time to do the things that we enjoy more often, and we are not left picking up after everyone. As well, having good manners prepares children for the future, because it teaches them to be considerate of others. Having good manners also bolsters their self-esteem.

If you have kids, after looking at the age appropriate chore chart, what chores have you decided you can get them started on? How about their manners?

_____

_____

_____

_____

It takes enormous amounts of patience and repetitive practice to teach our children to remember their manners and do their chores, so the lesson is ours too! How do you think they will handle making mistakes in the future if you are patient while teaching them now?

_____

_____

_____

_____

For a time, money can be tight in a firefighter household and with your partner working long shifts, most of the budgeting, shopping, and other monetary maintenance will likely fall to you. Money management can be another source of household stress, but handled properly this, too, can be overcome.

Do you think any of the suggested ways to make extra money are interesting/of use to you?

_____

_____

_____

_____

What are some of your own ideas about how to bring extra money into your home?

_____

_____

_____

Have you thought of investing in the stock market or in real estate? Why or why not?

_____

Fire Wife Companion Guide

Are you good at budgeting, or do you find it a challenge?

After reading through some ideas on how to save money, was there anything you'd like to try?

What are your own ideas on how to save money?

Do you have money-saving suggestions for date night, children's play-dates, clothes, or entertainment?

_____

_____

_____

Do you find purchasing groceries to be one of your bigger expenses?

_____

_____

You don't have to have it all to have a happy home since a happy home mostly comes from the simple and soul-satisfying things that create contentment: warm feelings, good memories, traditions and conversations.

Take some time to think about some of your favourite memories and what made them feel so special to you.

_____

_____

_____

_____

_____

Fire Wife Companion Guide

Who are some of your role models and mentors for building a family and friendships? If you could write an, "I learned from the best" editorial, who would you write about? If you'd like, write a letter of honor to the person who has inspired you, including why. You can send it to them or keep it to yourself.

Dear,

_____

_____

_____

_____

_____

_____

_____

_____

_____

_____

TARA McINTOSH

Do you have a favorite recipe you remember having at a friend's house when you were little? How about a favorite dish from your childhood home? Can you recreate it, or make it your own?

_____

_____

_____

_____

_____

_____

_____

_____

_____

_____

Standing Strong Tips Chapter Seven:

- Explore Happy Home Energy Practices From Around the World: Hygge from Denmark or Ikigai from Japan as Examples

- Declutter Your Home and Calendar to Make Room for Abundance, Peace & Pleasure

- Make an "Absolute Yes" List and an "Absolute No" List to Free Up Your Time for More Joy & Purpose

- Use This Space to Set More Standing Strong Goals

CHAPTER EIGHT

You Matter

"Your imagination is your preview of life's coming attractions."

~ Albert Einstein

YOU AREN'T JUST a Fire Wife, but a person who has a life all your own. You also have a heart that needs to be filled and a bucket list that needs completing! In this chapter, we are going to continue your timeline by taking a look at what you want out of life going forward. This begins with taking stock of your natural skills, your natural abilities, and the legacy you'd like to leave. But first, let's reflect on how you feel about a few things first.

FOLLOW YOUR GOALS AND DREAMS

What does "a life of your own" while being committed to your responsibilities look like to you?

_____

_____

_____

_____

How do you think your persistence in pursuing your dreams while navigating your partner's shift work will pay off for you down the road?

_____

_____

_____

Do you believe in the old saying, "timing is everything?" Do you have examples from the past when you realized you experienced "perfect timing?"

_____

_____

_____

YOU ARE GIFTED

What are your natural gifts and talents? To identify them, think about what comes easily to you.

_____

_____

_____

_____

_____

_____

What are you passionate about? To discern your passions, identify what you can spend hours doing and time just seems to fly by.

_____

_____

_____

_____

To fine-tune our natural gifts and talents, author Malcom Gladwell of the book 'The Outliers' says that it takes at least 10,000 hours to master something. Does this amount of time surprise you? How does it make you feel knowing it takes this long to master your gifts and talents?

_____

_____

_____

_____

Is there something you are currently doing for work or volunteering for that you are not passionate about?

_____

_____

_____

_____

Has status or money ever clouded your authentic dreams and desires?

_____

_____

_____

How much do you think you would accomplish if you focused solely on your natural gifts and talents, putting them to work in a compatible profession or volunteer position?

_____

_____

_____

_____

CELEBRATE YOUR FUTURE—CREATING A VISION

Have you ever written down a vision for your future?

_____

_____

_____

Have you created a vision board, a vision wheel or scrapbook of your dreams? Have any of those dreams come true?

_____

_____

_____

_____

_____

Having started on your timeline in Chapter 6, how would you like it to look going forward with respect to your life? Feel free to add as many decades as you like. What would you like to do, see, or accomplish? How would you like to live? What dreams would you like to pursue? Either work with the timeline provided, or make a bigger, more detailed one in your journal.

_____

_____

_____

_____

_____

_____

_____

_____

_____

_____

_____

_____

_____

_____

_____

_____

_____

_____

_____

_____

_____

_____

_____

When you create a vision of what you'd like your future to be, you're making decisions and setting your intention. What decisions for your life would you like to firmly make going forward? Think about all aspects of your life: health, personal growth, career, relationships, family, creativity, happiness, social life, and finances.

Fire Wife Companion Guide

_____

_____

_____

_____

_____

_____

_____

_____

When you close your eyes, how do you envision a beautiful life for yourself 5, 10, 15, and 20 years from now?

5:_____

10:_____

15:_____

20:_____

What are you doing and who are you surrounded by?

_____

_____

_____

_____

_____

_____

It is important to look ahead and map out your dreams, but it is just as important to look back over your life. Take the time to remember what dreams you had and what you did to manifest those dreams. If you didn't take the time to manifest those dreams, maybe it's time to take a look at them again.

Let's get started by organizing your scrapbook or vision board. When creating a vision for your life, be very detailed. Feel it too! It has been said that when you can feel the emotions of what you want in your life, they will come to you. I've reprinted the questions I asked in the Fire Wife book, about creating a vision for your life. Take some time to answer the questions to begin the process and start cutting or printing pictures for your scrapbook or vision board:

What is the vision you have for family?

_____

_____

What is your vision for friendships?

_____

_____

What do you feel called to do?

_____

_____

_____

_____

What charities would you like to be part of?

_____

What would be your ideal career or job?

Would you like to travel? Where?

What kind of a marriage would you like?

How much money would you like in the bank ten years from now?

_____

_____

Where would you like to live?

_____

_____

What creative ideas would you like to bring to light?

_____

_____

Health-wise, how would you like to feel?

_____

_____

What would you like to have accomplished? By what age?

_____

Do you have any "fantastical" goals (write a book, become a teacher, own your own business)?

What character traits would you like to improve on in order to make your dreams happen?

What would you like to learn (a new language, sewing, how to crochet)?

When creating your vision, pick your personal slogan, motto, mantra, or poem; something that inspires you from your favorite writers. Think about what philosophies you love, or what life laws encourage you.

HAVING NO REGRETS: AN EXERCISE IN FORESIGHT

Take some time to picture yourself as a 99-year-old woman. Then take some time to look back over your life. What will you regret in life if you don't do it?

_____

_____

_____

_____

What would you like to accomplish or do that would make you feel proud of yourself, satisfied and abundant when you are 99?

_____

_____

_____

_____

_____

What did you think about the cranky character Harriet in the movie '*The Last Word*' trying to construct a "good obituary"?

_____

_____

While it might feel uncomfortable to think about, what would you like your obituary to say?

_____

_____

_____

In looking back over your life, have you lived your values? Were you true to yourself? Have you lived your passions?

_____

_____

_____

Did you create community among strangers and people you loved? Have you made amends with any of those people? Did you spend quality time creating good memories with people you love?

Fire Wife Companion Guide

_____

_____

Did you fulfill your bucket list and use up all of your gifts and talents?

_____

_____

_____

What would help you to begin (or continue) to live a life that you are proud of? It's never too late to be what you might have been; don't let your mistakes hold you back. What fresh start would you like to have in your life?

_____

_____

_____

One way to discover the path you are meant to be on is to remember what you loved doing as a child. People have said that this is when we are at our most authentic.

What were your passions and interests when you were young?

_____

_____

_____

Did you know what your calling was early in life, later in life, or are you still looking?

_____

_____

_____

How do you like to spend your free time now, especially when you have no restrictions or time constraints?

_____

_____

_____

_____

To get an even better idea of what it is you would like to do in life, ask yourself what fulfills you:

I am fulfilled when I've accomplished:

_____

_____

I am fulfilled when I am around:

_____

_____

I am fulfilled when I do:

_____

_____

I am fulfilled when I spend my time:

_____

_____

_____

To achieve your dream, you just need to start somewhere. Remember the one phrase I learned over a period of two hours in Paris? Imagine if I'd learned one phrase a week for 20 years—I would have known plenty of French when I visited my dream destination. The lesson, I realized, was to just do a little something toward your dream every week and leave it at that. Don't judge it, don't feel guilty, don't let other people's expectations about what you need to accomplish throw you off. If you do something each week toward your goal, you will have 52 of something by the end of it! Whether it be writing a book, learning a new language, or working at a fitness program, patience and perseverance will pay off.

Using the space below, write your intention for what you would like to learn this week and then every week after that for an entire year. If you like, you can expand on this in your own journal.

_____

_____

_____

_____

_____

_____

Time for some R-Therapy: Retreat, Rest, Restore, and Relaunch. Have you ever retreated so that you could restore your heart and soul? It does take courage to do, because so many people tug at our time. It is, however, absolutely necessary to know when to take a sabbatical. I remember one of my son's elementary school teachers took a several-month sabbatical every 5 years to refresh her mind and get a new perspective on her life and her career. We all need to settle and restore our souls. Realizing that she knew what she needed, she would return to her students happy, enthusiastic, and eager to teach.

Not retreating to restore your heart and soul will lead to burnout. When I was burned out, I completely lost my zeal, creativity, and ability to dream. The only way to come back even better is to retreat so you can rest.

Can you relate to R-Therapy?

_____

_____

_____

_____

Have you ever taken the time needed to Retreat?

_____

Did you need to explain this to family and friends?

_____

_____

_____

Did they confuse your need to Rest with something more serious?

_____

_____

_____

Whenever we take the time to Rest, we always come back raring to go. What activities do you find Restore your heart and soul?

_____

Fire Wife Companion Guide

_____

_____

_____

Do you make time to Retreat without feeling guilty?

_____

_____

_____

_____

Knowing that it will be better for everyone, including yourself, how can you let go of guilt in order to understand that this is a very important thing to do for yourself?

_____

_____

_____

_____

Having read through the different "dreamer" stories, are there any people you respect, are inspired by, and admire for their personal dream story?

_____

_____

_____

_____

_____

_____

What about you? What have you done that has inspired those around you?

_____

_____

_____

_____

Going back to your natural gifts and talents, what do you find you do really well, even though you have had no formal training? Where are you perhaps not certified, but definitely qualified (such as being a cook, mechanic, builder, writer, speaker, or investor)?

_____

_____

_____

_____

_____

In addition to fine-tuning your natural talents, what formal education or courses could you take to help you with your dream?

_____

_____

_____

Every bit of experience counts. You may not know it yet, but nothing goes to waste. How do you think the experience you are accumulating now will help you in the future for your big-picture dreams?

_____

What can you do today to help you toward your dreams? Is there a phone call you can make? A venue you can book? Try not thinking about it too much. Just do it! You will feel so proud of yourself when you do.

The Ultimate Two-Step Plan: receive a good idea; make it happen. You don't get your good ideas from the status quo: you get them from inspiration. The word "inspire" is derived from Latin origins to mean, "to breathe or blow into (you) (from) divine or supernatural agency or power."

What are some of the best ideas you've ever had?

Did you find they came out of nowhere, or was there some inspiration for them?

How do you explain this? Do you agree with the definition of inspiration, that it doesn't come from the status quo but rather from a divine or supernatural agency to you?

When you get a really great idea, do you keep it a secret for a while or do you share?

_____

When you haven't shared your dreams with encouraging or trustworthy people, have you felt discouraged or silly for it?

_____

_____

What about when you share it with encouraging people?

_____

_____

_____

Have you ever followed your inspiration through to manifestation? Explain what you achieved.

_____

_____

_____

How often do you let negative thinking, fear, or other people's criticism get in between steps one and two of the Two-Step Plan?

_____

_____

_____

_____

Going forward, what would encourage you when you feel this "stuff" getting in the way?

_____

_____

_____

_____

_____

Learning to cheer yourself on is necessary for getting to where you are going in life. It requires confidence and a solid vision (or "faking it until you make it"). Learning how to detach from unconstructive criticism is also a great thing to learn.

Are you pretty good at picking yourself up and carrying on?

_____

What would help you to focus on running your race and living your dreams instead of being side-tracked?

_____

_____

_____

_____

You will be faced with challenges, but perseverance will always get you there. What words can you say to yourself or what memories can you recall about your courage that will cheer you on as you work toward your dreams?

_____

_____

_____

Are you good at encouraging yourself when faced with pushback or criticism, or do you need help from others?

_____

Does your partner support you?

_____

_____

If you have trouble cheering yourself on, what encouragement do you need (books, lectures, support group) to help you to stay the course?

_____

_____

How can you deal with unconstructive criticism from other people, including your firefighter?

_____

_____

Doing your due-diligence in any venture is essential. One cannot go into any project without a plan. Have you done your due-diligence with respect to your dream?

Have you showed your partner a business plan or verbally told them the steps you plan to take so that they understand what it is that you want to do?

Do you put undue pressure on yourself to hurry up and get stuff done?

What would help you to regain a sense of peace when you feel pressured?

In addition to working toward your dreams, what other responsibilities do you have in your life?

_____

_____

_____

How do you feel when you realize that many successful people didn't even get going until later in life?

_____

_____

_____

How do you relate this to the Law of Order?

_____

_____

_____

Regrets are a waste of time. Starting now, how can you live your life so that you will have no regrets? How can you squeeze lots of adventures, discoveries and accomplishments into your life?

What would help you to do that?

_____

_____

_____

_____

_____

It's time to stand strong in your personal story. In looking over your timeline, take some time to reflect on what have you overcome, accomplished, spearheaded, or stood for that helped you to grow, change your life, or boost your confidence. Consider also how your life lessons have shaped your life's story, and how your unique experience could inspire others.

After reading through Tara Stroup's story, what odds have you overcome to become better than you were before?

_____

_____

_____

_____

Wherever you might be right now, envision an amazing future with you, your partner, and family. Write down what you would like to see in your future with those you love.

_____

_____

_____

_____

_____

Are you able to trust that things will work out in the long run?

_____

_____

Do you realize how powerful your thoughts are in creating your future?

_____

_____

_____

When, in the past, were you worried about your future, only to see now that things worked out even better than you thought?

_____

_____

_____

_____

Imagine that you are teaching a class about life to a group of young students with the focus on accomplishing goals and achieving dreams. Having read through "My Top Ten Truths for the Dream Journey" and keeping your own life experience in mind, what truths for the dream journey would you like to add to the list of ten?

_____

_____

_____

Have you ever set goals and made plans to accomplish and achieve your dreams, only to have had those plans unexpectedly interrupted or changed? What would you say to your young students about dealing with these changes?

When have you moved from your intended Plan A (need Another plan) to plan B, C, or even D (Best Choice Darling) to, in hindsight, realize that it turned out better than you thought it would?

What are some of the lessons learned or personal growth you've garnered from having to become adjustable and flexible with life's unexpected changes?

_____

_____

Do you trust the universe's plans for you?

_____

_____

Spend some time in this last portion of the workbook to remember and focus on your strengths.

You are the architect of your life, and it is within your power to change it anytime and in any direction you would like. After reading through Fire Wife, *what changes, choices, and decisions about your relationship, your life and your dreams would you like to make?*

_____

_____

_____

_____

_____

_____

_____

_____

_____

_____

_____

Having a good relationship with your partner is very important, but having a good relationship with yourself is even more so. Take some time to think of what would help you to stand strong and stay committed to:

Yourself and your needs?

_____

_____

_____

_____

_____

Your growth?

Your 'Amour Propre?'

Your relationship?

Fire Wife Companion Guide

_____

_____

Your life?

_____

_____

_____

_____

Your dreams?

_____

_____

_____

_____

_____

If you and I could have a chat together, what part of 'Fire Wife' would you say helped you the most?

_____

_____

_____

_____

_____

In a paragraph or in a few short sentences, write down on this last page what chapters in 'Fire Wife: Standing Strong in Your Relationship, Your Life, and Your Dreams' were helpful to you. What tools and skills would you like to implement into your life and relationship?

_____

_____

_____

_____

_____

Standing Strong Tips Chapter Eight:

- Take the Time to Map Out Your Life & Bucket List

- Comparing Yourself to Others Is Like Comparing Roses. Run Your Own Race and Put Your Blinders On

- Just Start Where You Are

- Learn to Cheer Yourself On

- Study People You Admire or Whose Steps You'd Like to Follow In

- Character is Destiny

- You've Got This!

- Use This Space to Set More Standing Strong Goals

CREATING THE FIRE WIFE BOOK CLUB

FOR MANY YEARS, particularly as a young mom, I belonged to many different types of groups to explore my creativity. Mostly I joined writing groups, which came complete with good-hearted women, cups of tea, and endless support and encouragement. That is my hope for *Fire Wife* and this *Fire Wife Companion Guide*: that you get to know your fire wife sisters by coming together to provide one another with the sustenance that comes from shared experiences.

If you would like to gather other fire wives for a book club or discussion group, here are some suggestions for success and fun!

GATHER YOUR GROUP AND DECIDE WHERE TO MEET

When seeing who would like to participate in your Fire Wife Book Club, send out an email to a mix of people: some of whom you know well and some you don't. I find that having participants whose significant others share the same shift as yours to be helpful, since if you have children, you can pick a book club night when your partner will be home with the kids.

Usually, a book club works well if there is a facilitator that keeps the discussions flowing. If you are initiating the book club, maybe it can be you who facilitates the book club in your home. Or possibly everyone in the club can take turns hosting and facilitating. The facilitator will simply walk the group through a few key, chosen questions during the time you are together, and any thoughts and ideas people had about the chapter that week.

DECIDE HOW OFTEN YOU'LL MEET, FOR HOW LONG, AND WHEN

There's a lot to cover in this book, but not every question needs to be answered in the workbook or discussed as a group. Start by choosing a few key questions, or allow individuals in the group to offer up questions that resonated with them.

However, if you and your group would like to go through each question, the book club would probably take much longer to complete. Decide in advance if your group will meet once a week, bi-weekly, or once a month and for how long. There is no need to rush—figure out a time period that works best for the most people.

Sometimes one question or topic will really resonate with the group and will need to be discussed for much longer than the time you've booked for your gathering. Therefore, being flexible and adjustable is key when meeting with your group.

As for the duration of the book club gathering, I've always personally loved two to two and a half hours. The additional half hour allows for a break to have refreshments. You can also set up a private social media account where you can socialize and discuss the book in between your gatherings.

Having a good time is the priority in any book club. Enjoy the book and work through this guide at a happy pace that suits your group. This is not supposed to feel like homework. Focus on gathering and supporting one another to create community.

SET BOUNDARIES

When you send out your email, make it clear that this is a positive atmosphere (no gossiping about others) and that your Fire Wife gathering is for camaraderie: to encourage, share, and learn.

If you have to, set a timer to allow for each person to speak about their question for five minutes or so. This allows everyone to have equal time to discuss the book and the questions in the guide.

Remember that listening to one another is better than trying to fix a situation or offer advice. Go with the flow, relate and encourage, but respect what season each person is in their fire relationship.

Create an atmosphere of trust. As I pointed out, there can be a lot of gossip back at the fire hall. Set firm boundaries that honor those who do need to speak up about private things so that they can get the help they need from other fire wives. Trust is vital at this gathering.

HAVE SOME FOOD AND FUN!

Food is center to fire life, so of course there's got to be food! Whether it be a full-on potluck dinner, appies, or a big pot of soup, food, friends, and fun make book clubs a cherished occasion that create great memories. Consider having everyone bring a copy of their recipe to share with the group. Who knows? Maybe you'll have enough for your own fire wife cookbook.

Here's to books! Here's to fire life! Here's to *bon appétite!*

www.ingramcontent.com/pod-product-compliance
Lightning Source LLC
Chambersburg PA
CBHW071833080526
44589CB00012B/1002